FIREFIGHTING IN TYNE & WEAR

An Illustrated History

FIREFIGHTING IN TYNE & WEAR

An Illustrated History

RON HENDERSON

TEMPUS

To all the officers and personnel of
Tyne & Wear Fire & Rescue Service
past and present.

First published 2007

Tempus Publishing Limited
The Mill, Brimscombe Port,
Stroud, Gloucestershire, GL5 2QG
www.tempus-publishing.com

British Library Cataloguing in Publication Data.
A catalogue record for this book is available from the British Library.

ISBN 978 07524 4274 7

Typesetting and origination by Tempus Publishing Limited.
Printed in Great Britain.

Contents

Introduction

The present day Tyne & Wear Fire & Rescue Service was established on 1 April 1974 as the Tyne & Wear Metropolitan Fire Brigade. The establishment of the new brigade was a direct consequence of the Local Government Reorganisation Act. The Act saw county borough fire brigades and other public services become incorporated into new countywide authorities. Under the new system the former fire authorities of South Shields, Sunderland, Tynemouth and the joint Newcastle & Gateshead Fire Service would all cease to exist as independent entities when they were incorporated under the Tyne & Wear banner in 1974. There were also changes to the surrounding counties; north of the River Tyne four fire stations from Northumberland, Gosforth, Newburn, Wallsend and Whitley Bay were transferred into Tyne & Wear. From Durham, fire stations at Birtley, Chopwell, Hebburn, Swallwell and Washington also came under the umbrella of the new Tyne & Wear body. Today, Tyne & Wear's seventeen fire stations provide fire cover to a population of 1.08 million people over an area of 540 square kilometres.

At the turn of the twentieth century only major cities and boroughs had professional fire brigades (they were usually attached to the police force). In the rural and smaller urban districts fire brigades were often not provided, and there was no legislation to compel these councils to provide firefighting resources. In order to avoid being forced to pay for the service, some councils argued that annual fire losses were actually less than the cost of providing a fire engine. Despite this, many councils did provide suitable protection for their citizens and municipal assets. In the years leading up to the outbreak of the First World War Gosforth, Newburn, Whitley Bay, Wallsend and Jarrow Urban District Councils all had professional fire brigades. Some councils contracted out responsibility for their protection, usually to either the surrounding brigades or the Durham and Northumberland Collieries Fire & Rescue Brigade. During the Second World War all of the nation's fire brigades were nationalised and came under the controlling authority of the Home Office. This came with the proviso that when peace returned the brigades would once again be under county council control. This did eventually happen but with subtle differences to the pre-war arrangements. In 1948 new county fire authorities were formed that incorporated all of the pre-war urban and rural district fire brigades but the county borough fire brigades reverted back to their pre-war status. This situation remained until the Reorganisation Act of 1974.

Upon the formation of the new brigade in 1974 nineteen fire stations were transferred. From the former Newcastle & Gateshead Fire Service came their station and headquarters at Pilgrim Street in Newcastle city centre. The Newcastle & Gateshead service also transferred the Fossway Fire Station at Walker, the West End Fire Station at Arthur's Hill, Westgate Road, and the Gateshead Fire Station on Dryden Road. Sunderland was covered by four fire stations: the headquarters at Dun Cow Street and sub-stations at Fullwell, Grindon and Tunstall. There were two fire stations at South Shields – the main one at Keppell Street and a sub-station at River Drive – and from the small Borough of Tynemouth came their single fire station at Preston Road. The remaining nine fire stations were those from Durham and Northumberland.

At the stroke of midnight on 31 March 1974, control of these fire stations, along with their personnel and equipment, was transferred to Tyne & Wear Metropolitan Fire Brigade. In essence the new brigade began operations with a wide assortment of fire engines. They ranged in age from brand new to twenty-six years old, and naturally there was little standardisation in such a hastily assembled fleet of vehicles. The new fleet was made up in large part of AEC-make vehicles, which were used in Newcastle & Gateshead, Sunderland and South Shields. Equally common were ERFs from both Newcastle & Gateshead and Sunderland. The appliances transferred from the county stations were of Commer and Bedford make.

Considering this eclectic range of vehicles, an early priority for the new brigade was the acquisition of new fire appliances to replace the obsolete ones and bring in some degree of uniformity. One of the main advantages of creating one brigade to cover the wider area was the ability to purchase large batches of vehicles of standard design, and within the first decade most of the old appliances had been sold and replaced by a new fleet of Dennis-built vehicles. A similar rationalisation has since taken place regarding the fire stations. During the brigade's thirty-two years many of the older fire stations have been replaced by new community fire stations, while changes in fire cover have meant that some stations closed altogether. Both Whitley Bay and River Drive suffered this fate, and other stations have amalgamated or re-sited. The brigade's headquarters at Pilgrim Street, in the centre of Newcastle, closed in 2006 and the fire appliances were moved with those from the West End into new premises at Colby Court, Rye Hill. The headquarters' staff relocated to a new facility at Barmston Mere, Washington, in company with the new brigade training centre.

This book sets out to illustrate and briefly describe the fire engines that have operated within the Tyne & Wear region, including those from previously independent services that have come under the control of the Tyne & Wear Fire Brigade. It includes examples from the earliest days of hand and horse-drawn carts to the latest developments. Fire engines are machines, not just methods of transporting personnel to fires, and for this reason preference has been given to photographs that depict the fire engines in action. The human aspect and the personnel responsible for providing fire and rescue services twenty-four hours a day must not be left without mention, and it is hoped that this history will form a worthy tribute to all those involved in making the British fire service one of the finest and most illustrious of all organisations.

Acknowledgements

I would like to thank my fellow enthusiasts and the organisations, cited below, which have kindly allowed the reproduction of selected photographs, for which many thanks are extended and appropriate credit is given in the relevant chapters: the Chief Officers and personnel of County Durham & Darlington, Northumberland and Tyne & Wear Fire & Rescue Services for their unceasing co-operation and encouragement; Ian Moore, a fellow historian for over forty years; Neil Steel and the British Commercial Vehicle Museum Archives; Alexander Dennis and Surrey History Service for permission to reproduce the Dennis photographs; South Tyneside Library and the following individuals, who have all contributed in some way, for which the author is ever grateful: the late Dennis Barker, Bret Clayton, Ricky Senior, Arthur Smith, Norman Tarling and Trevor Welham.

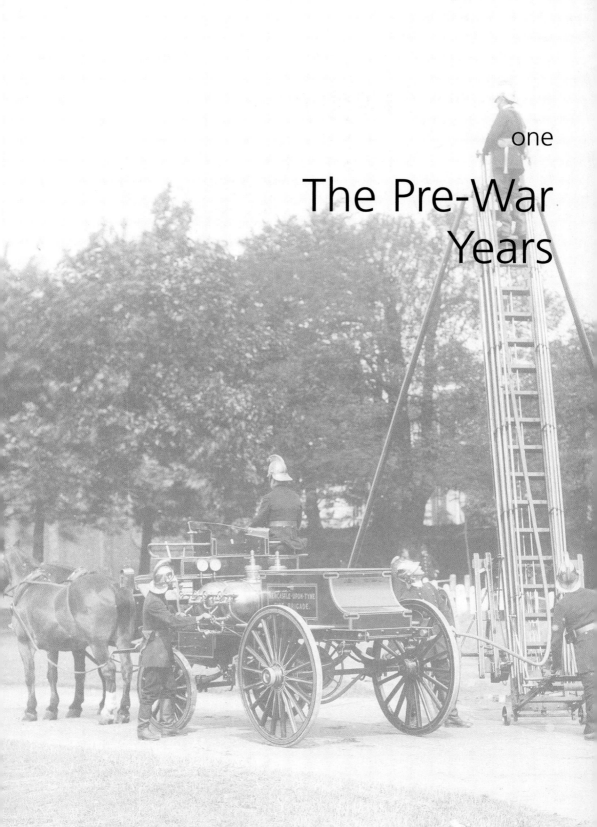

one

The Pre-War Years

Gosforth Fire Brigade, under the command of Superintendent Fred Coney (from Sutton in Surrey), was equipped with this hose cart until it acquired its first and only steam fire engine in 1908. Coney was the only paid man in the brigade at that time; the rest were council workers whose successors continued to man one of the fire engines at Gosforth right up until 1975.

In 1903 the Fullwell Parish of the Sunderland Rural District Council consisted of twenty-two part-time firemen and a manual fire engine and hose cart. Later they were equipped with this Merryweather hand-drawn 'chemic', which was basically a king-size soda acid fire extinguisher.

Early fire pumps were hand operated and required many men to man the handles that operated the pump. For this task they were paid with tokens, which were later exchanged for either money or ample supplies of beer. This Merryweather manual was used by South Shields Fire Brigade; it was of the style used by most fire brigades of the era. (Merryweather)

Both the Hylton and Ford Parishes, later incorporated into the Borough of Sunderland, were issued with combination hose and ladder carts, probably the earliest form of dual-purpose appliance. (Merryweather)

Tynemouth Fire Brigade, whose fire station was actually at North Shields, was equipped with this Merryweather portable steam fire engine and carriage, a rudimentary yet economical measure for combating fires in the borough. The type was later given the name 'Valiant', after one was sold to supply fresh water to Her Majesty's Ship *Valiant*. (Merryweather)

Gateshead Fire Brigade's equipment, in common with most of the borough fire brigades, was operated by policemen or 'fire bobbies'. As well as modern steam fire engines the town also operated this two-man Merryweather 50ft escape carriage. (Merryweather)

When the limitations of the system became apparent it was decided that horses were a better form of propulsion, particularly considering the increase in the size and weight of appliances. This hose tender at the Redbarns Fire Station was used by Newcastle City Fire Brigade and accompanied one of the brigade's steam fire engines.

Newcastle Fire Brigade, another police fire brigade, had this bigger escape tender built by John Morris of Salford. It could accommodate eight men as well as carrying a hose in the box under which the men were seated.

Above: The City of Newcastle also bought this Merryweather combined double-cylinder chemical fire engine, hose tender and fire escape. It featured a pair of soda-acid chemical fire extinguishers. Before someone came up with the idea of mounting the escapes onto horse-drawn equipment they had to be trundled to fires by hand. (Merryweather)

Opposite above: Gosforth Urban District Council bought this Shand Mason steam fire engine in 1905, proudly displayed with its crew outside the High Street Fire Station. During its eight years of service it only turned out eight times and was used in operation on only three occasions. The other occasions were either test calls placed by members of the council or times when the building in question was beyond help.

Below: Sunderland Fire Brigade operated this interesting escape tender with Shand Mason lattice girder escape ladder. The borough had their money's worth from this equipment, as the ladder was later mounted onto a motorised appliance and remained in service until 1961. (D. Barker collection)

Steam fire engines constructed by the now defunct London firms of Merryweather and Shand Mason were the most widely used types in the United Kingdom. This Merryweather Greenwich Gem was one of a pair operated by South Shields Fire Brigade that was delivered in 1894 and 1903. It is pictured here in the yard at the rear of Keppel Street. (South Tyneside Library)

This Shand Mason steam fire engine, pictured in 1898 at the Dun Cow Street Fire Station, was part of the Sunderland Fire Brigades force. At the time it was manned by twelve professional firemen and fifteen policemen. (D. Barker collection)

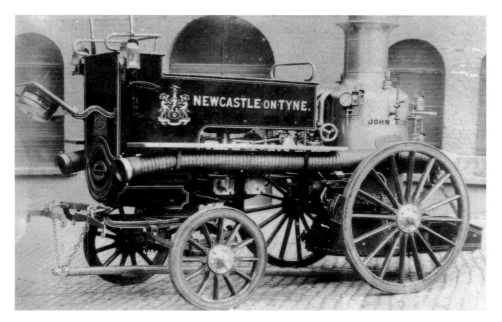

Named after John Reid, the chairman of the Fire Brigade Committee, this Merryweather Horizontal 'Greenwich' steam fire engine is pictured in 1903 outside the manufacturer's works at Greenwich. With a capacity of 759 gallons per minute it was one of four steam fire engines operating in the city at the time. (Merryweather)

To protect its industries on the banks of the River Tyne at Scotswood, including the major shipbuilding yards, the Armstrong Whitworth Works at Elswick invested in this powerful Merryweather fire float long before the municipal brigades considered acquiring such an asset. (Merryweather)

Prior to the Second World War many police fire brigades took on responsibility for operating a street accident ambulance service and billed the incumbent for their services. These two Crossley ambulances, pictured at the Waterloo Street headquarters, were part of the Newcastle City fleet.

There is no doubt where the firm of Tilling Stevens was based. One of the Newcastle Tilling Stevens vehicles was used to mount the brigade's first turntable ladder, an 85ft model manufactured by Braun. This appliance was later fitted with pneumatic tyres on the front wheels and was in service in the city until the war years.

One of the best equipped fire brigades in the north-east was the Northumberland and Durham Collieries Fire & Rescue Brigade. This service provided fire protection to all of the region's coal mines and associated properties, as well as being available to council fire brigades on a commercial basis. Their Scotswood Road Fire Station, pictured here, also covered the sprawling Vickers Armstrong premises across the road.

The fire station at Gosforth before a second storey was added. Superintendent Fed Coney is in the driving seat of the towns first motorised fire pump, a 1912 Dennis 'N' type. In the garage is the brigade's Hotchkis tender.

In 1922 Newcastle Fire Brigade purchased three petrol-electric Tilling Stevens fire engines to supplement the Dennis and Belsize vehicle bought earlier. This example was fitted with a demountable 300-gallon per minute pump; the big wheels at the rear were used to trundle the pump to a convenient water supply.

Newburn Urban District Council Fire Station, originally built for Spencers Steel Works, was passed to the Urban District Council when the steel works closed. The premises came under the jurisdiction of Northumberland County Fire Brigade in 1948 but in 1974 they passed into the control of the newly created Tyne & Wear Fire Brigade.

Many fire brigades operated hose tenders as an economical way of transporting hoses and personnel to fires. This 24hp Ford operated at Newburn until 1933.

As motorised fire engines became increasingly popular the old horse-drawn equipment was usually mounted onto a new chassis in place of the former hand or horse traction. Newcastle operated a pair of these Dennis vehicles to transport men and equipment. None was fitted with pumps. (Copyright: Alexander Dennis)

Following the delivery of the two Dennis escape tenders in 1916, Newcastle Fire Brigade standardised on Leyland fire engines, the first of which is pictured here before delivery. Unusually for the time, it was fitted with a windscreen. (BCVMA)

Wallsend operated a pair of Dennis 'N' type fire engines after it was decided to motorise the brigade. This one was the motor pump, the other was equipped to carry a wheeled escape and was not fitted with a pump. (Copyright: Alexander Dennis)

In 1931 Gosforth got rid of their old Hotchkis tender and mounted the body onto this new Guy Motors chassis, seen here at the wedding of one of the members of the brigade. Superintendent Jack Hann, who replaced Fred Coney, is the officer standing by the happy couple.

Whitley and Monkseaton Urban District Council Fire Brigade operated this Leyland pump escape until the war years. The registration number, now much sought after, was 'X6666'. (BCVMA)

The Dennis Ace fire engine was a popular choice for some of the smaller fire brigades, and for many years this particular appliance was the sole fire pump in the Borough of Tynemouth. A similar machine was later bought by Hexham Council. (Copyright: Alexander Dennis)

Trailer-mounted pumps were popular supplements to self-propelled pumps and hose tenders, Jarrow Fire Brigade acquired these two Dennis examples in 1931. (Copyright: Alexander Dennis)

This Leyland pump escape was the last appliance to be ordered by Sunderland Fire Brigade before the Second World War. It served the town until 1963 and throughout its service it operated with the old horse-drawn Shand Mason escape ladder. (D. Barker collection)

The small town of Gosforth operated a most efficient fire brigade and in 1938 it purchased this locally built limousine-type Bedford hose tender, finished in a lime green livery. Superintendent Jack Hann is on the extreme left.

In 1936 Newcastle ordered four new Leyland fire engines, one turntable ladder and three of these limousine motor pumps. These were the first enclosed appliances in the city and offered much greater protection from the weather than the open-cab 'Braidwood' style appliances. This one, pictured at Headlam Street in 1965, served the city for thirty years.

Two of the three Leylands have been preserved and in 2000 a reunion was arranged. The two vehicles were brought back to Newcastle and posed on the forecourt at Pilgrim Street where they last operated together over forty years before. Apart from the Tyne & Wear 'Keep Clear' sign there is little to suggest that the scene is a modern recreation.

Sunderland bought this locally built Bedford emergency tender (ET) in 1936, and it remained in service until 1960. It attended most fires in the borough, as for a considerable amount of time it was the only vehicle in the fleet with a two-way radio. It was known as the ET-Wireless.

This powerful looking appliance was aptly named the 'Big 4' by the manufacturers, Dennis Bros, of Guildford in Surrey. Delivered to the Borough of Wallsend in 1934, it is pictured here turning out from Wallsend Fire Station in 1948 after being transferred to the newly formed Northumberland County Fire Brigade. (NCFRS)

This small Leyland FK1 motor pump posed on the forecourt at Keppel Street, South Shields, served the town for almost twenty years between 1934 and 1953. Even at this late stage fire crews were still travelling to and from fires on precarious open-bodied vehicles.

Many years elapsed between Gateshead Fire Brigade's purchase of a trio of solid-tyred Leyland Fire Engines and the acquisition of this brass-adorned Leyland by the town in 1938. After the war it passed into the combined Newcastle & Gateshead Joint Fire Service fleet. (BCVMA)

two

Post-War Changes

GXA 756

Above: This Austin escape-carrying unit, which served during the Second World War, was later fitted with a front mounted Barton pump. It operated from Whitley Bay Fire Station until the station received its new post-war Commer multi-purpose pump in 1954. The large building on the left is the Royalty Cinema on Gosforth High Street, in whose car park the fire brigade's workshop was situated. (NFRS)

Opposite above: Felling Fire Station was originally established by the National Fire Service during the Second World War, and it later became the site of the north-east regional fire service training school. In the immediate post-war years the station housed two former NFS appliances and a pre-war Stockton-on-Tees Dennis Light 4 motor pump. (CDDFRS)

Opposite below: Three London Fire Brigade appliances that had served in the Blitz were transferred to Durham County Fire Brigade in 1948 for use as training appliances at the regional training school at Felling. One of two 1933 Albion motor pumps is pictured here at Felling soon after going into operation. (CDDFRS)

Many former National Fire Service appliances were rebuilt after the war in order to gain more years of service pending the release of new chassis. This Sunderland Austin major pump was converted from a former escape-carrying unit in 1951 and remained in service in the borough until 1960. (D. Barker collection)

This pre-war Bedford emergency/salvage tender of Newcastle & Gateshead Joint Fire Service was acquired from a private owner in Wooler, Northumberland, and operated for the brigade until 1968. After the war it operated from both Gateshead and Pilgrim Street and is pictured here in 1966 at a flooded cellar incident at the Turbinia Public House, Fossway, directly opposite the site of the future Fossway Fire Station.

The livery of this chequerboard Commer Q25 appliance (masquerading as a mobile control point) and its location suggest that it was assigned to the Newcastle & Gateshead Joint Fire Service. The venue was a large civil defence exercise in June 1952, which operated under the premise that both Gateshead and Newcastle had been the victims of a nuclear attack. (B. Clayton collection)

Hebburn's original fire station was situated in Hedgeley Road in a requisitioned old house with garages at the rear for housing the appliances. This 1949 scene, after the premises came under the jurisdiction of Durham County Fire Brigade, shows a former NFS Fordson pump escape and a Bedford heavy unit appliance. (CDDFRS)

Architecturally, fire stations came in all shapes and sizes. Birtley Fire Station was situated at Cottage Farm on the Great North Road. The kitchen and storeroom of the cottage were converted to house its sole appliance, a former Stockton-on-Tees Dennis Light Four appliance. (CDDFRS)

Wallsend's firemen parade in front of the Chief Fire Officer and other dignitaries in 1948. The firemen are still attired with wartime steel helmets. In the background is the station's wartime Bedford heavy pumping unit. (NFRS.)

Newcastle & Gateshead Joint Fire Services fireboat *Francis*, another wartime estuarial type, was berthed at Wincomblee, Walker, and manned on a full-time basis. An expensive resource, it was funded by a combination of Northumberland County Fire Brigade, Durham County Fire Brigade and the Home Office, but it was withdrawn in 1957 when repair costs could not justify its continuation.

The line-up at South Shields on the return of the brigade to local authority control consisted of a mixture of two former National Fire Service appliances and their pre-war open Leyland motor pump. Within two decades the brigade would have a standardised fleet of Merryweather engineered AEC vehicles.

In 1953 the Rex Hotel in Whitley Bay suffered a major fire to the upper floors, requiring the Whitley Bay crews to seek reinforcements from Tynemouth, who sent their 100ft turntable ladder and a major pump. Here both Tynemouth appliances accompany Whitley Bay's wartime pump escape as crews prepare to make up equipment, having once again 'won the battle'.

After the end of the Second World War the civil defence was resurrected and training exercises were regular occurrences. Northumberland County Fire Brigade staged this big exercise on the premises of the Swan-Hunter and Wigham-Richardson shipyards at Wallsend in 1950.

The fire service stock in the immediate post-war years consisted of standard wartime fire engines and those pre-war appliances that had survived the war. Pictured here at Wallsend in 1952, alongside the station's newly delivered Commer multi-purpose pump, Hexham's pre-war Dennis Ace was in use as a service reserve.

Newburn Fire Station operated Northumberland County Fire Brigade's last pre-war appliance, a 1937 Leyland limousine that was delivered that year to the Newburn Urban District Council. Pictured in 1953 reversing into the appliance room at its home station, it was sold in 1962 whereupon it gained a new lease of life as a recovery vehicle with Andersons Coaches, Westerhope.

Durham County Fire Brigade's workshop personnel, under the command of Transport Officer George Strangeways, had this former NFS hose-laying lorry rebuilt into an Emergency-Foam/Salvage Tender for use at Hebburn. It remained in service there until 1966. The workshop personnel were firemen and tradesmen, and as well as repairing and rebuilding appliances they were also required to man an operational appliance. (CDDFRS)

Both Northumberland and Durham modernised several of these wartime Austin auxiliary towing vehicles, fitting them with small water tanks and hose reels. For many years they would form the mainstay of the brigade's rural fire stations. The 'B14' on the Coventry Climax trailer pump of this Durham appliance denotes that it was based at Dunston. (CDDFRS)

Sunderland Fire Brigade operated one of these Leyland TD7 turntable ladders with a Merryweather 100ft ladder. They were part of a batch ordered by the Office of Works in the months leading up to the Second World War. The single cab for the driver signifies its origin as a bus chassis. (D. Barker collection)

Neighbouring South Shields Fire Brigade received a similar example during the war years. In common with most redundant fire engines the appliance came to a sad end at the hands of the scrapman's burner. (N. Tarling)

Many efforts were made to recruit the approved quota of auxiliary firemen and women. This is one such recruiting display arranged at Hebburn by Durham County Fire Brigade in October 1951. As well as Hebburn's appliances there is an old Bishop Auckland steam fire engine and Durham City's 60ft turntable ladder. (CDDFRS)

All fire brigades underwent an annual inspection by one of His Majesty's Inspectors of Fire Service. This 1950 Inspectorate exercise was at Moor Court, Gosforth. Inspector Percy Booth, on the right, takes notes as appliances from Gosforth and Pilgrim Street are put to work.

The first fire engine acquired by the Newcastle & Gateshead Joint Fire Service (formed in the immediate post-war years) was this Commer foam tender/pump. It was built by the brigade's own workshop staff, saving the ratepayers £2,000 in the process. During the Royal Show at Newcastle it was based in a temporary fire station on Newcastle Town Moor *c.*1962. (I. Moore collection)

The Newcastle & Gateshead Joint Fire Service expressed a preference for diesel-engined fire appliances, and bought the first of their three AEC Regent vehicles in April 1952. Pictured before delivery, this appliance worked for almost all of its operational life at Gateshead. (Merryweather)

In Durham County the brigade bought one example of Dennis's successful Rolls-Royce-powered F12 series pump escapes. The appliance was allocated to Hebburn Fire Station where it operated for almost twenty years. Similar appliances were delivered to Sunderland and Tynemouth Fire Brigades. (CDDFRS)

Northumberland County Fire Brigade operated a standardised fleet of Commer appliances for its full-time fire stations, and Gosforth took delivery of this Miles-bodied water tender in 1952. The appliance was originally equipped with a wartime Sigmund-Morris trailer pump with a similar pump mounted inboard. This appliance was in service at Gosforth for over twenty years.

The first new appliances ordered by Sunderland Fire Brigade were from Dennis Bros of Guildford, Surrey. Here the second and third new deliveries, both Dennis F12 vehicles, are pictured on the forecourt at the town's Central Fire Station at Dun Cow Street. (D. Barker collection)

South Shields Fire Brigade opted for diesel-powered fire engines and bought this 9.6 litre AEC Regent with Merryweather fire equipment, including a 1,000 gallons per minute pump, in 1951. After twenty-two years of service it was sold to Newcastle & Gateshead Joint Fire Service for use as a driver-training appliance and thereafter was sold to a private owner who preserved the appliance. (Merryweather)

As well as the water tenders Northumberland ordered several multi-purpose pumps, basically water tenders equipped with a 50ft wheeled escape. Wallsend's Fire Station took delivery of the prototype, which is pictured there shortly after delivery. Identical appliances were also allocated to Gosforth, Newburn and Whitley Bay.

Another Home Office Inspectorate exercise, this time at Newburn, who had just received their new Commer multi-purpose pump. Northumberland's Chief Fire Officer William Muir and Home Office Inspector Percy Booth watch as the crew undertake a drill with the wheeled escape on the forecourt in 1954. (NFRS)

There were two fire boats on the River Tyne, part funded by each of the brigades that covered areas bordering the river. This is the South Shields vessel, a former National Fire Service estuarial type fireboat. Built at Chertsey, it was originally intended for service on the Thames and the Mersey.

Tynemouth Fire Brigade also ordered a pair of Dennis F12 pumping appliances. The second of the pair, delivered in 1953, featured a rear-mounted 1,000 gallons per minute pump, as opposed to the amidships-mounted pump on the town's earlier Dennis. This appliance, pictured at a cornfield fire at Billy Mill in 1971, served for over twenty years. After passing to Tyne & Wear in 1974 it was ignominiously scrapped at Byker.

Many fire brigades converted wartime-standard appliances into up-to-date limousine vehicles. This Austin heavy pump unit, of Newcastle & Gateshead Joint Fire Service, seen here working at a Home Office Inspectorate exercise at Benton, was one such conversion.

Newcastle & Gateshead Joint Fire Service bought three AEC Regent fire engines. The last one, delivered in 1954, was later sold to Winterton Hospital in Sedgefield, County Durham, for use by the hospital fire brigade. The appliance is seen here returning from a fire at Grove Street, Elswick; at the time it was on reserve duties in the West End.

South Shields Fire Brigade received their second AEC Regent dual-purpose appliance in 1953 to match a previously delivered sister. Pictured on the forecourt at Keppel Street in 1968 some fifteen years after delivery, it was still in front-line service and looking as good as new.

Merryweather fire engines on AEC chassis were dominant in the north-east in the 1950s and 1960s, and following the earlier Regent fire engines several of the brigades (including South Shields) based their standardised fleets on the successor, the Merryweather Marquis. This South Shields appliance was delivered in 1957 and served at the River Drive station.

During the 1950s there were frequent local and national campaigns to recruit auxiliary firemen and women. Frequent public displays were held to encourage volunteers to enrol. A selection of the fleet, all painted in an olive green livery, are displayed at Wallsend in 1955.

Regular firemen participated in the recruiting campaign; at Wallsend firemen here demonstrate one of the new AFS bikini units to members of the public. The inflatable bikini raft could carry three portable pumps, one of which was used as the motive power for propelling the craft.

As well as recruiting campaigns, training exercises formed a large part of the duties of auxiliary fire service personnel. Firemen from Hebburn set to work with an inflatable dam and two green goddesses during one such exercise at Sutherland Quay, Tyne Dock.

In the early 1950s Wallsend Fire Station received a pair of new Commer fire engines which were to serve the borough for over twenty years. The town's second example, a water tender dating from 1953, turns out from the Lawson Street Station shortly after delivery.

Following the AEC Regent diesel fire engines of Newcastle & Gateshead Joint Fire Service, the brigade stayed loyal to AEC and Merryweather and bought the first of several Merryweather Marquis fire engines. Pictured at the manufacturer's before delivery, the appliance was assigned to Headlam Street, Byker, in 1958, but did not stay there long. (Merryweather)

Gateshead Fire Station received a new Merryweather Marquis fire engine in 1961. It is seen here undergoing its pre-delivery inspection at the manufacturer's works at Greenwich before making the long journey north to Newcastle. (Merryweather)

Of the original three Newcastle & Gateshead Merryweather Marquis fire engines, Arthur's Hill Fire Station in the West End of the city received the second example, which was pictured whilst attending a fire at Fawdon on Guy Fawkes' Day, 1968.

Gosforth Fire Station, on the High Street (part of the Great North Road), was established in 1903 and was unusual in that the fire station was situated through a tunnel at the side of the council chambers. The station's multi-purpose pump hurtles out of the archway onto the Great North Road on another errand of mercy. This appliance was one of the hardest worked in the region.

Drills are part of the daily routine of firefighters. Here a crew from Gosforth get to work with the station's 50ft Bayley wheeled escape. The tunnel to the right gave access to and from the brigade's workshops in the Royalty Cinema car park, from where the mechanics manned the second fire engine during weekdays.

South Shields Fire Brigade's fleet consisted almost entirely of Merryweather appliances mounted onto AEC chassis. In 1962 the borough received this smart combined emergency/salvage tender that also contained facilities for operating a ground communications role in a fire. After delivery it was fitted with two roof-mounted illuminating red and white chequered domes to signify its control function. (Merryweather)

In 1961 Tynemouth Fire Brigade bought a Bedford foam tender on the strength of the construction of a new oil tank storage farm at Howdon. Equipped with a 300-gallon foam tank, for many years the appliance was unique in being the first and only naturally aluminium-coloured appliance in the Tyne & Wear region.

Right up until the mid-1960s Newcastle & Gateshead Joint Fire Service used an old wartime towing vehicle as a recovery unit. It is pictured here struggling up Pilgrim Street in the process of towing a disabled Gateshead appliance to the workshops at Arthur's Hill.

At one time the entire fleet at South Shields was based on AEC appliances with Merryweather fire engineering, as seen here in the rear yard at Keppel Street during the annual Home Office Inspectorate exercise. (D. Barker collection)

Perkins Engines entered the firefighting field in 1963, producing a 'Mars' portable gas turbine fire pump of 500 gallons per minute capacity. South Shields Fire Brigade bought an example; one of its many uses was that it could be mounted onto this boat which could then deputise for the larger estuarial fire boat should it be put out of action for any reason.

This rather lengthy Bedford fire engine was a foam carrier delivered to Sunderland Fire Brigade in 1963, where it operated from the brigade's headquarters before moving to Grindon. It was never fitted with a pump but carried numerous drums of foam compound. It is pictured here at Gateshead in 1980 when in use as a driver-training vehicle.

Appliances of the Newcastle & Gateshead Joint Fire Service were unique, with their overall deep maroon livery enhanced by vermilion lockers and mudguards, black roofs and black-edged silver lining. This livery was carried over from the pre-war years and this Gateshead pump escape shows it off to good effect. (T. Welham)

Sunderland's Rolls-Royce-powered Dennis fire engines were replaced by Merryweather Marquis diesel appliances, a pair of which operated from the brigade headquarters at Dun Cow Street in the town centre. One of the pair was equipped with a 50ft steel escape ladder. (D. Barker collection)

Sunderland's first post-war fire engine was sold in 1967 to Sunderland Airport for use as a fire and rescue crash tender. Some conversion work had been undertaken, such as the removal of the full-length bottom locker to give additional ground clearance and the fitting of a larger water tank. The appliance was operational when this picture was taken in 1968.

South Shields Fire Brigade took delivery of this new AEC Merryweather Marquis Series 6 water tender in 1963 at a cost of £5,380. Unlike the other pumping appliances in the fleet it had no facilities for carrying a wheeled escape.

Merryweather produced a very successful line of turntable ladders and were pioneers in hydraulically operated units. Sunderland Fire Brigade took delivery of this 100ft hydraulic turntable ladder in 1961 and similar appliances were also ordered by Newcastle & Gateshead, South Shields and Tynemouth Fire Brigades. (D. Barker collection)

What would have been the last AEC pump for Newcastle & Gateshead Joint Fire Service, a deluxe version of the previous Merryweather appliances, was ordered from Angus Fire Armour of Westgate Road. Assigned to Headlam Street, both the station's appliances are in attendance at a television set on fire at Hotspur Street, Byker.

In common with all of Northumberland's full-time fire stations, Newburn was equipped with a pair of Miles-bodied Commer fire engines. During busy times standby cover was provided at overstretched fire stations, as demonstrated by Newburn's water tender reversing down the arch at Gosforth in 1968.

When delivered in 1965 this impressive Dennis F107 emergency tender of Newcastle & Gateshead Joint Fire Service was the biggest and most comprehensive of its type in the region. Complete with front-mounted winch, it was available on request to all of the surrounding fire brigades. Based at Pilgrim Street, after the reorganisation it served at various Tyne & Wear fire stations, notably Gosforth and Fossway. (N. Tarling collection)

The same year as the new emergency tender was delivered, Headlam Street's major pump, the brigade's first Merryweather Marquis, was written-off on Guy Fawkes' Night whilst proceeding to a serious fire at Richardson's Leather Works, Elswick. This accident prompted the brigade to place an order for a similar appliance. (I. Moore collection)

In 1969 Gosforth's original water tender escape was exchanged with an identical model from Hexham to try and bring the mileages between the busiest and least-used appliances closer together. The former Hexham machine thunders up Station Road, South Gosforth, early one morning on its way to a fire at Longbenton. This particular incident occurred only shortly after its transfer.

Merryweather's AEC Regent fire engines were fitted with a torsion bar stabiliser to the rear wheels to enable smooth cornering at greater speeds. This is seen to good effect in this picture as one of Newcastle's Regent major pumps hurtles round the corner into Fawdon Park Road on its way to a fire in 1968.

Many of Gosforth's turnouts were to fires in Newcastle & Gateshead Joint Fire Service's area. One such incident shows a pair of appliances from Newcastle's West End station arriving at a chimney fire at Kirkwood Drive, North Kenton, in the winter of 1967. Upon arrival the Gosforth appliance would be released. In this type of situation three fire engines for a chimney fire was the norm.

The same street six months later. This time in the height of the summer, Gosforth's water tender, manned by the station's part-time firemen, is pictured parked up whilst the crew extinguish another chimney fire. In this pre-central heating era householders often had to light the coal fire in order to get hot water, hence the chimney fire on what was a very hot day.

Sunderland opted for Merryweather Marquis vehicles in preference to the earlier Dennis pumps. These were the brigade's first diesel-powered fire engines and their second Marquis, assigned to Dun Cow Street, is pictured here in company with a similar type on Guy Fawkes' Night. On this occasion a Grangetown resident's chimney had caught fire.

Pilgrim Street's Merryweather Marquis in company with a similar appliance from Byker. They are pictured here arriving at a fire at the old Prudhoe Street Dole Office near the Haymarket. Merryweather habitually removed the chassis maker's plate from the front of the appliance and replaced it with their own badge, which incorporated a 'By Appointment' cipher and the company name.

Northumberland County Fire Brigade's Wallsend Fire Station received the prototype Commer/Miles multi-purpose pump in 1951. It immediately proved a tight fit in the pre-war fire station. It operated as the first turnout appliance at Wallsend for over twenty years.

In 1968 the Wallsend appliance was damaged following a road accident on Rosehill Bank. It was subsequently rebuilt with a more modern front assembly which belied its age. It is pictured a long way from home, just about to hurtle through Fawdon Railway Crossing on its way to a grass fire whilst providing standby cover at Gosforth.

Gosforth's 'white watch', pictured in Regent Road in 1967, filling up the 400-gallon water tank of the water tender escape after undertaking some hydrant tests. The spectator on the cycle later enrolled in the brigade and rode that very fire engine with those very firemen. Forty years later he wrote this book.

Elm Grove, Fawdon and Gosforth's water tender escape attends yet another summertime chimney fire. Shortly after this photograph was taken two more fire engines from Newcastle's West End Fire Station arrived, releasing the Northumberland crew.

The first in a long and successful line of ERF fire engines was acquired by Newcastle & Gateshead Joint Fire Service in 1967 and made its debut at the brigade's centenary parade the same year. A spectacular-looking appliance, with performance levels to match, it operated from the start at Pilgrim Street. Claimed to be the fastest fire engine in the fleet when delivered, it was fitted with wide-track single rear wheels, but these were later changed to twin wheels.

The same year two innovative 'mini fire squirts' were introduced for gaining access to the new shopping precincts, notably the Eldon Square indoor shopping centre in Northumberland Street. Here one of the pair is dwarfed by Newcastle's prototype ERF fire engine. The pair of 'minis' was the equivalent to one conventional-sized pumping appliance.

One of the minis, pictured at a fire at George Street, Scotswood, soon after going operational. The third crewmember rode in the open, behind the crew cab. The experiment with the mini was not a success, and after extensive trials at the brigades four fire stations they were withdrawn and the idea was not developed any further.

Both of the mini squirts arrive at a kitchen fire at Sturdee Gardens, Jesmond, in 1967. An appliance from Northumberland County Fire Brigade's Gosforth Fire Station also attended the incident. The narrow dimensions of the cab prevented the firemen from getting dressed en route to the fire.

Newcastle & Gateshead Fire Service held a centenary parade in the summer of 1967 to commemorate one hundred years of organised fire brigades in the City of Newcastle. As well as the parade a display of firefighting was held at Newcastle Exhibition Park.

Newcastle City, and later the joint fire service, got thirty years of service from the pre-war Leyland appliances. The penultimate one to be withdrawn is pictured here in a scrapyard alongside the Redheugh Bridge. Years later it was discovered at a coach dealer's at Birtley and bought by Tyne & Wear Fire Brigade, where personnel from Tynemouth Fire Station have been steadily engaged in restoring the machine to its original condition. (I. Moore collection)

Fire calls to British Paints Ltd, Portland Road, Newcastle, required a pre-determined attendance of four appliances from Pilgrim Street, one from Headlam Street and a foam tender from Gateshead. Headlam Street's major pump heads the line-up of appliances for just such a call in 1968.

Turnouts at Pilgrim Street were always exciting affairs, with firemen running into the main A1 and stopping traffic to allow the appliances a quick exit. This did not happen on this occasion as the whole fleet was turning out and all the firemen were scrambling onto the engines.

Another turnout from Pilgrim Street, on a wet Sunday afternoon in the autumn of 1968, this time for a leaking gas pipe in the Shieldfield area.

Newcastle's West End Fire Station in 1969 and both appliances, Whisky 1 and 2, turnout on another errand of mercy. This station was usually the busiest of the four Newcastle & Gateshead fire stations. It closed in 2006 when a new station was opened at Colby Court.

Purpose-designed foam tenders were not common, but South Shields Fire Brigade ordered this AEC-Merryweather appliance when the new oil tank farm was being constructed at 'The Lawe' on the banks of the River Tyne. It is pictured here at Gateshead where it was transferred after the 1974 amalgamation.

Sunderland's main fire station headquarters at Dun Cow Street in 1965 showing three AEC appliances and their Bedford/Miles emergency tender. The emergency tender was the only appliance in the fleet to be fitted with a Francis siren. (D. Barker collection)

A pair of AFS green goddesses on the sea front at South Shields drafting water from the sea during a training exercise. The green goddess on the left has been fitted with a non-standard electric bell and dwarfs the mini pick-up unit from South Shields Fire Brigade.

Sunderland were allocated three green goddess emergency pumps for use by the AFS. This Sunderland goddess was pictured a long way from home, at Kielder Forest, Northumberland, where a camp had been established for use by AFS personnel at weekends.

The AFS were adept at moving large quantities of water over long distances and often used quite innovative methods in the process. At the Groyne at South Shields, crews set up a water relay with the aid of three light portable pumps and a bikini raft.

On 31 March 1968 the illustrious Auxiliary Fire Service was stood down and disbanded. At Gateshead Fire Station, an AFS green goddess awaits collection and removal to a Home Office Transport Store, an event that was repeated with all AFS appliances throughout the country.

Following the disbanding of the AFS, Tynemouth Fire Brigade bought one of their two redundant green goddess emergency pumps and converted it into a road accident vehicle. Finished in an all-over yellow livery, it was the only yellow appliance in the north-eastern region.

Northumberland County Fire Brigade bought two green goddesses, both of them four-wheel-drive versions, one of which operated as a reserve at Gosforth. Although it was re-sprayed red the driver still had to rely on the forward-facing orange blinker lights and hand-operated bell to warn traffic. The height of the machine made it a tight fit in the entrance to the appliance room.

During the 1960s the local fire stations were regularly called out to the West End of Newcastle. Pictured here, two of Newcastle's pumps from the West End Fire Station have been called to a fire in a derelict house at Prospect Place.

Newcastle's Angus Fire Armour major pump from Headlam Street and Gateshead's salvage tender attend a flooded cellar at the Turbinia Public House, Fossway, in 1968. This incident occured directly opposite the future site of the Fossway Fire Station.

Whitley Bay received their new multi-purpose pump in 1954 to accompany a water tender previously delivered. The appliance is seen turning out in 1970 to a fire in the cloakroom at Boots Chemists on Whitley Road.

Having been a victim of man's great enemy – fire – the next call from Boots Chemists was about a flooded cellar. The brigade's water tender was despatched and a portable pump lowered into the cellar to drain it.

A garden shed fire at Low Teams, Gateshead, in 1968 was attended by an appliance from Durham County Fire Brigade's Swallwell Fire Station and Gateshead's pump escape.

South Shields Fire Brigade took delivery of this Merryweather Marquis water tender in the winter of 1963. It is pictured here the day after the SPD warehouse fire at Newcastle Road, which was one of the borough's biggest fires. Twenty pumps from all over the region attended the fire.

Hebburn Fire Station operated a pair of 1950s Dennis appliances, a six-cylinder F8 model and a larger eight-cylinder F12 type. Both are pictured here ascending Bill Quay Bank on their way back to the station from a fire at Marconi's works on the banks of the River Tyne. During their time at Hebburn they were known as 'father and son'.

All of Northumberland's water tenders were rebuilt to house two new Coventry Climax light pumps. They were housed in a full-width enclosed locker in place of the wartime Sigmund-Morris pumps. The Gosforth appliance begins its return to the station from a cornfield fire at Newbiggin Hall Estate in an era when a large part of the weekly routine was defined by the painting of the tyres, as seen in this photograph.

Newcastle's West End pump ladder is pumping for all its worth during a major fire at John B. Bowes' paper warehouse on Westgate Road. By this time the traditional wheeled-escape ladders had been replaced by 45ft light alloy ladders. (I. Moore collection)

Another of Newcastle's major fires occurred at Firestone Tyres, Westgate Road, in July 1969. Travelling from across the River Tyne, Gateshead's pump ladder pumps water onto the fire from a Blenheim Street hydrant.

Newcastle's biggest peacetime fire occurred on the night of 30 November 1969 at Callers Department Store in Northumberland Street which caught fire when loaded with Christmas goods. Two Newcastle & Gateshead appliances and a water-tender escape from Northumberland are parked up in Northumberland Street at the height of the fire.

At the rear of Callers on John Dobson Street, Byker's pump escape is engaged in pumping water onto the fire on what was a bitterly cold night.

This Ford emergency/salvage tender marked a milestone in the history of Newcastle & Gateshead Fire Service. It signalled the end of the brigade's traditional maroon and red livery. Instead it featured every colour but maroon. The overall colour was red, the front grill white, the roof black and a broad yellow stripe was painted on the side. (NGFS)

The next year another Ford fire engine was delivered, this time in a plain red livery (apart from the black roof). This was a high expansion foam tender ordered to replace the first post-war fire engine that Newcastle & Gateshead Fire Service bought, the old Commer foam tender which was by then operating from the West End.

The Callers fire was one of the first fires that Newcastle's new 85ft 'Simon Snorkel' appliance attended. Seen on acceptance trials at Gateshead in 1969, this machine featured a CCTV camera in the cage which relayed pictures to a television screen housed in a locker. It was the first fire engine in the region to be fitted with reverse FIRE signs on the front.

In August 1969 Whitley Bay's popular nightspot, the Sands Club, above the bus station on Park Avenue, was gutted by an early morning fire. Whitley Bay's water-tender escape was still in attendance at daybreak, whilst crews turned over debris looking for hot spots.

In both Northumberland and Durham the station officer in charge of each fire station was on call from home at weekends and evenings. The station officers were provided with official transport at these times. This Commer Cob van was the steed of the station officer at Gosforth, and is pictured with the retained crew in 1967 at a hearth fire at Bridge Park.

Newcastle & Gateshead Joint Fire Service bought two Merryweather hydraulic turntable ladders. The second one, delivered in 1966, was the last AEC to be bought by the brigade and is pictured assisting Northumberland County Fire Brigade at the old Pearl Cinema in Wallsend.

Pilgrim Street was assigned this Series V Merryweather Marquis dual-purpose appliance, from where it operated with a wheeled escape when first delivered in place of one of the AEC Regents. It is pictured at a fire in a derelict building at Forth Banks in 1967 running as a major pump. The metal bracket at the rear of the appliance is the escape mounting gear.

Newcastle's prototype ERF fire engine in attendance at a large fire at Davisons Paper Sales, Corporation Street, in 1968.

The Regent fire engines were still giving sterling service during the late 1960s. The first example was pictured in 1968 at a fire at Bells Court, Pilgrim Street. Although the base livery was supposed to be maroon, these appliances had a brown cast to them and because of this they were known throughout the brigade as 'chocolate boxes'.

Sunderland's second Marquis Series VII is shown at Fullwell carrying a Merryweather 50ft steel escape ladder. In these appliances the rear crewmembers sat facing backwards for safety reasons. This photograph was taken in the last week of the Sunderland Fire Brigade's existence, after which it was subsumed within the newly formed Tyne & Wear Metropolitan Fire Brigade. (D. Barker collection)

Following withdrawal from service the appliance was sold to a coach company at Sacriston, County Durham. Here it was converted into a recovery vehicle and gave many more years of service.

South Shields Fire Brigade also received one of the new Series VII Merryweather Marquis fire appliances. After the reorganisation of 1974 it served at Washington, with the original wheeled-escape ladder replaced by a 45ft aluminium ladder.

In 1969 Whitley Bay Fire Station was operating this water tender, formerly of Berwick and still carrying that name on the door. The vehicle was standing in for the station's regular water tender that was temporarily out of service. The appliance never underwent the conversion that the Miles water tenders had and at this late stage it was still equipped with a trailer-mounted pump.

This was the line-up at Tynemouth's sole Fire Station in 1972: a major pump, pump/hydraulic platform, foam tender and turntable ladder. The nearest appliance had been in continuous front-line service for twenty years when the photograph was taken.

Land Rover fire engines were rare in the north-east of England, but Sunderland Fire Brigade bought this vehicle in 1971, primarily for towing a trailer-mounted foam monitor. It also deputised for the emergency tender when required, hence the front-mounted winch. Note the varnished wooden doors of Sunderland's Central Fire Station. (D. Barker collection)

The acquisition of the prototype ERF fire engine prompted Newcastle & Gateshead Fire Service to order further examples, and in 1971 a pair of these HCB-Angus-bodied appliances were delivered for Pilgrim Street and the West End. Pilgrim Street's vehicle is seen attending a training exercise at the site of the new Freeman Road Hospital.

In the 1960s a new type of fire engine appeared: the pump/hydraulic platform vehicle. This was basically a water tender with a hydraulic platform device. In 1971 Tynemouth Fire Brigade became the first brigade in the region to acquire one.

Newcastle & Gateshead Fire Service soon followed suit, and in 1971 they purchased a pair of smart ERF pumps with 50ft elevating hydraulic platforms and day-glo striped booms. Bodied by the same company as the Tynemouth example, the individual specifications ensured the two vehicles looked totally different.

Newcastle & Gateshead, Sunderland and Tynemouth all opted for ERF fire engines to replace their older AEC machines. Illustrated here is one that Tynemouth received in 1972. It was one of the last north-east appliances to be fitted with the traditional, but increasingly obsolete, fire bell.

When the Chief Fire Officer of Rochdale was appointed to the same position at Sunderland, he brought some of his own ideas with him. He ordered this ERF emergency tender, which was identical to one previously ordered by Rochdale Fire Brigade, even down to the livery. (D. Barker collection)

Sunderland Fire Brigade had the distinction of purchasing the last escape-carrying fire engine in the Tyne & Wear Region. Delivered in 1971, it operated for only one week with the wheeled escape and was pictured during that time outside the central Fire Station at Dun Cow Street. The inclement weather had prompted the fitting of skid chains on the rear wheels. (D. Barker collection)

The last fire engine bought by the South Shields Borough Fire Brigade before the reorganisation of 1974 was this Jennings-bodied Dodge 50ft pump/hydraulic platform appliance, delivered in 1972. It was later sold to Cleveland County Fire Brigade.

Some fifty years lapsed between Newcastle & Gateshead Joint Fire Service buying pumping appliances from the famous Dennis Co. In 1973, the last complete year of the joint brigade's existence, it bought one new Dennis water tender. This vehicle was to provide the basis for the standardised fleet of the soon-to-be-formed Tyne &Wear Metropolitan Fire Brigade. (I. Moore collection)

Sunderland Fire Brigade's last new appliance, and the last ERF to be delivered to any north-eastern fire brigade, was not actually delivered until after the formation of Tyne & Wear Metropolitan Fire Brigade. Therefore it never appeared in Sunderland Fire Brigade livery. It is pictured here in 1979 when operating from Washington.

Both fire stations at South Shields were incorporated into Tyne & Wear. River Drive Fire Station, on the banks of the River Tyne, operated one pump, with the crew manning the fireboat which was attached to a buoy just behind the fire station.

Two fire stations manned on a part-time basis became part of the new Tyne & Wear establishment, Chopwell and Birtley. The two Birtley Carmichael-bodied Karrier water tenders on the right, together with the fire station, were transferred from Durham County Fire Brigade on 1 April 1974. (I. Moore collection)

three

Reorganisation

The line-up at Pilgrim Street during Newcastle & Gateshead Fire Service's last week. The two nearest appliances, both ERFs, were finished in the brigade's red livery, whilst the turntable ladder and emergency tender are still displaying the original maroon and red livery. They were both later re-painted red.

Newburns Fire Station, incorporated into the Tyne & Wear organisation in 1974, was in a rather hazardous location as far as turnouts were concerned. The building was still in use in 2006 as a car repair workshop but the railway bridge had been removed.

The most modern fire station to be inherited by the Tyne & Wear Fire Brigade was at Tunstall on the south side of Sunderland, from where one of the former fire appliances hurtles out of the station on its way to a cornfield fire in 1974.

When Tunstall Fire Station was first opened in 1974 it was manned by two crews. The second appliance, also a former Sunderland Borough machine, turns out here to the same cornfield fire. Corrosion has resulted in the rear bodywork being re-panelled in natural finish aluminium.

For many years Durham County Fire Brigade operated with Bedford vehicles, nine of which were transferred to Tyne & Wear in 1974. This 1970 HCB-Angus water tender was formerly based at Hebburn and is pictured in November 1977 at a warehouse fire on the Tyne Tunnel Trading Estate.

Hebburn Fire Station operated this Miles-bodied Bedford emergency tender, one of a pair ordered by Durham County Fire Brigade to replace the converted Fordson vehicles. The Hebburn appliance became part of the Tyne & Wear fleet in 1974.

This South Shields 100ft turntable ladder, based on an AEC Mercury chassis, is acting as a water tower at a disused school fire at Argyll Street, Hebburn, in March 1984 after the merger. The appliance was to be found in a Durham vehicle dismantler's in 2006.

Also inherited by Tyne & Wear Fire Brigade, the livery of this Newcastle & Gateshead turntable ladder of similar make was soon replaced by a traditional red livery. The appliance is seen in action at Scotswood Road, Newcastle, in July 1982, when part of the former Vickers Armstrong factory was destroyed in a blaze.

This small Bedford water tender, built by Hampshire Car Bodies in 1960, was one of several serving with Durham County Fire Brigade. Assigned to the part-time fire station at Chopwell, it was inherited by Tyne & Wear in 1974, in whose livery it is pictured in 1977 shortly before it was sold.

One of the priorities of the new brigade was the replacement of obsolete fire engines. A former South Shields AEC water tender awaits disposal in the yard at Arthur's Hill, Newcastle. The end for such vehicles was often an inglorious one in a scrapyard.

This former Newcastle West End appliance gained a reprieve and was granted further service as a recovery vehicle with Eno's Circus. The gaudy colours do little to hide its former occupation.

Less successful was the former Northumberland Commer that was transferred to Tyne & Wear's Wallsend Fire Station in the final days before the merger. It was scrapped at Shepherds, Byker, in 1977.

In the same yard, accompanying other former Northumberland fire engines, was Hebburn's foam tender. This vehicle had been used as a driver-training vehicle. At twenty-three years of age it was one of the oldest appliances inherited by Tyne & Wear.

Having languished swivelling around a buoy in the River Tyne for many years, the South Shields fire boat was moved to a berth at Tyne Dock, prompted by the closure of the River Drive Fire Station shortly after the merger. (A. Smith)

Not long after the merger of 1974, Tynemouth's pump/hydraulic platform appliance overturned during a rain storm whilst responding to a call from the Rex Hotel. Fortunately there were no serious injuries to the crew.

The wrecked Tynemouth appliance in the yard at Newcastle's West End Fire Station in 1977. The vehicle was rebuilt and placed back into service, remaining operational until it was sold in 1983.

The first new fire engines bought by Tyne & Wear Metropolitan Fire Brigade were a batch of ten water tenders from Dennis Ltd, based on the company's F109 chassis. They were diesel-engined with automatic transmission and rear-mounted pumps. The first of the batch is pictured at Scotswood Road, Newcastle, attending a fire at the old Vickers Armstrongs Factory.

Specifications for housing suction hoses were omitted from the first generation Dennis appliances, so they had to be strapped to the roof. All of the early Tyne & Wear Dennis machines had reversed FIRE signs, a roof-mounted monitor and rear-facing crew seats. This one was based at West Denton when pictured during a fire at North Shields in 1985.

The 1976 batch of new pumps had updated front assemblies, as this example hurtling out of the yard at Gateshead in 1986 shows. The six-bay fire station in the background, built by Newcastle & Gateshead Fire Service, was demolished in 2005 and replaced by a new building on the same site.

Six Dennis F131 appliances were delivered in 1976, further standardising the fleet. Gateshead operated this appliance, which had made its way over the Tyne Bridge to attend a fire at Clayton Street in Newcastle city centre in 1979.

The first new turntable ladder for Tyne & Wear was from Dennis, with coachwork by Carmichael & Sons of Worcester, the agents for the German 100ft Magirus ladder. Operating from Pilgrim Street, it was one of two such ladder appliances called to this disused warehouse fire at Scotswood Road.

In 1977 six further Dennis F131 appliances were delivered. One came to grief in 1982 in a collision with another appliance whilst en route to what turned out to be of a malicious call. Fortunately, none of the crew was seriously hurt and the appliance was repaired and put back into operation.

The brigade changed from Dennis in 1977 when this Shelvoke emergency tender with Carmichael bodywork was delivered for Hebburn Fire Station. Later operating from Fossway, it was written off in an accident in February 1987 and scrapped at Dunston six months later.

There were six 'STY' Dennis water tenders delivered in 1978, the last two of which were re-registered with a later year's registration number. The first of the batch was allocated to Fossway and is photographed turning out in February 1987.

In 1981 this lengthy incident command unit was delivered to Tyne & Wear for West Denton
Fire Station. Based on a Dennis Dominator bus chassis with coachwork by Angloco of Batley,
West Yorkshire, it was one of the biggest of its type in the country. Equipped for undertaking
communication duties, it also featured a conference area, toilet and even the proverbial kitchen
sink. It is pictured during a major incident at Newcastle Central Railway Station on the last day of
November 1988.

Tyne & Wear Fire Brigade took delivery of the last of a long line of 'F' Series appliances manufactured by Dennis Ltd of Guildford, Surrey. One of the batch of three attends a house fire at Melbury Avenue, Heaton, in 1980.

A complete change from Dennis appliances took place in 1981 when Tyne & Wear bought this Shelvoke SPV/Carmichael water tender for evaluation. Stationed at Tynemouth and then Hebburn, it was later sold to the Irish Civil Defence. The notion of illuminated fire signs and roof monitors had disappeared with the delivery of this appliance.

The fourth and last Shelvoke appliance of Tyne & Wear was another emergency tender, built with special limitations to fit into Wallsend Fire Station. Upon delivery it was assigned to Fossway and in fact never served at Wallsend. With ample room in the appliance room at its new location, it was returned to the body builders and fitted with a rear body extension.

The same appliance after the conversion to add an extension to the rear bodywork. A large lead plate was affixed to the chassis behind the rear wheels to improve the stability of the vehicle. It ended its days operating from Pilgrim Street, by which time it had been embellished with red and yellow chequered high-visibility panels.

That same year the brigade's first new foam tender was delivered to replace the outdated versions inherited in 1974. When delivered, the appliance had an unpainted aluminium body but it was re-bodied in 1988 into the format illustrated in this picture. The appliance operated from Whitley Bay for many years and was sold in 1993.

Many fire brigades adopted a system of demountable units, where various modules containing specialised equipment could be transported to an incident and left at the scene, thus enabling the vehicle to be used elsewhere. One such unit, equipped with a canteen unit module and alternate salvage tender module, was stationed at Tynemouth.

After Dennis ceased production of the 'F' series fire engines, the replacement models – the steel reinforced cab 'RS' and 'SS' series vehicles – formed the basis of the company's next generation of fire engines. Tyne & Wear bought their first example in 1982 and based it at Tynemouth, from where it operated until becoming a driver-training vehicle in 1990. Withdrawn in 1995, it was sold for further service in County Cork, Eire.

There were three of these Dennis DF133 appliances with German-built Magirus 100ft ladders in the Tyne & Wear fleet. The first of the three, delivered in 1984, was assigned to Tynemouth and is seen here on a Sunday morning in October 1985 operating at a major fire at a North Shields upholsterers.

The brigade's second new foam tender was delivered in 1984, and although the body was made by the firm that made the earlier one the chassis chosen was Dennis. It is pictured in its original state in 1986 at an exercise at Team Valley Trading Estate, Gateshead. The vehicle was later re-bodied and finished in an overall red livery.

Having taken delivery of one Dennis 'RS' appliance in 1982, several batches of 'SS' vehicles with tilt cabs were delivered. This 1985 vehicle operated from West Denton and acted as support pump to the command unit; it is seen here in this capacity at Washington in November 1989.

Carmichael and Sons of Worcester supplied the bodies on the 1985 batch of new Dennis pumps for Tyne & Wear. Previous orders had Dennis-built bodies. There were five in the batch, and this picture shows Fullwell's vehicle at Newcastle Road in 1986 when a petrol tanker crashed and overturned. After disposal the appliance gave further service in the City of Dublin.

In 1988 a series of Dennis appliances with bodywork by Fulton & Wylie of Falkirk were delivered. They were the first in the brigade to feature strobe lights and electronic sirens. This one operated from Fossway Fire Station.

Fossway Fire Station in the East End of Newcastle pictured in 1988. Only the two appliances on the right were operational. The other appliances consisted of a schools education unit and a driver-training appliance. The station closed in 2005 on the opening of a replacement station at the top of Shields Road. (T. Welham)

The original Wallsend Fire Station during its last week of operation. The cramped confines were replaced by a new community fire station at Hadrian Road in March 1989.

Gateshead Fire Station showing a line-up of Dennis appliances. Opened in 1961 the station was demolished in 2005, and with the aid of the Private Finance Initiative a replacement was built on the same site. (T. Welham)

Hebburn Fire Station was opened in July 1965 by Durham County Fire Brigade and replaced a station on Hedgeley Road. In this 1988 view the establishment was home to two pumping appliances and an emergency tender. Later an ambulance was housed in the station. (T. Welham)

After many years of buying Dennis fire engines, the second decade of Tyne & Wear Fire Brigade saw the acquisition of standardised Volvo fire engines for its pumping appliances. The first batch of five pumps and one emergency tender arrived in 1988. Washington's example is pictured at a corn stubble fire at Donwell in 1990. The appliance was later acquired by Tipperary Fire Service in Eire.

The first of three new Volvo emergency tenders was assigned to Hebburn in 1988 and transferred to South Shields the following year. There it remained until it was stood down in 1999. It was sold to Essex County Fire & Rescue Service in 2003.

Three rescue tenders based on American GMC chassis were bought between 1988 and 1990, with one of their roles being to tow special equipment trailers and the fireboats. This Fossway example was sold in 1997 to an Irish fire brigade. (T&W F&CDA)

Opposite above: Two small fireboats were acquired for operation on the north-east's major rivers: the *Tinea*, based at Fossway for the River Tyne, and the *Vedra*, based at Sunderland for the River Wear. They were originally mounted on trailers and towed to launching sites by the rescue tenders. (T&W F&CDA)

Opposite below: From 1989 Volvo fire engines were built by a new entrant to the fire engine scene, Excalibur Ltd. Between 1989 and 1996 the brigade received thirty-one examples. From the first batch Gateshead's example is seen at the disused Forty-Bond warehouse at The Close, the scene of several big fires.

The delivery of the Volvos resulted in the brigade's earlier Dennis deliveries being withdrawn. The redundant vehicles were parked at the rear of the West End Fire Station prior to removal to auction.

One of the major fire risks in the Tyne & Wear region is Newcastle International Airport, where regular training exercises are held. Five Volvo water tenders line up at the rendezvous point in December 1997, awaiting the commencement of just such an exercise.

After many years of using turntable ladders as water towers and rescue appliances, Tyne & Wear bought their last one in 1995, from then on preferring to buy aerial ladder platforms instead. Still operating the last such appliance in 2006, it was fitted with a Magirus ladder and was operated from Fossway Fire Station. (T. Welham)

As well as the turntable ladder at the Fossway, the other rescue appliances in Tyne & Wear consisted of a pair of Bronto aerial ladder platforms supplied by a firm in Finland. Capable of reaching to heights of 32 metres, they are based at Gateshead and Fullwell.

Gateshead Fire Station received this Volvo curtain-side operational support unit in 1997, a special appliance that was ordered to replace the two foam tenders. The Moffat Mounty forklift truck on the back was used for loading and unloading the containers of foam. (T. Welham)

In 1982 funding was made available to two Fire Safety Units for educating school children on the dangers of fire. Two new Dodge lorries were ordered to convey the demountable pod system to sites where the module could be left *in situ* and the vehicle utilised elsewhere. In 1997 the unit received this new Volvo chassis.

After operating from the same site for almost a hundred years, Gosforth's original High Street Fire Station and its two appliances, pictured here in March 1989, were transferred to new premises in 1990 in the grounds of the former Collingwood Clinic on Jubilee Road.

As well as the plethora of Volvo fire engines, small batches of Dennis Sabre 1,000-gallon per minute pumping appliances with coachwork by Emergency One were delivered in 1998 and 1999. Tynemouth's example is seen attending a training exercise at the Tyne Tunnel in 2001.

Four more Volvos were delivered in 1999. West Denton's example was despatched on the long journey to Washington in company with the station's incident command unit when fire ripped through the derelict Cape Insulation Factory in June 2003.

When the American rescue tenders were withdrawn, depriving the fireboats of their towing vehicles, a redundant water tender was converted into a boat tender to convey the Fossways boat to the launching site at Newcastle Quayside. The boat was launched with the aid of a turntable ladder. (T. Welham)

The Dennis boat tender and the fireboat *Tinea*, were later replaced by a Volvo prime mover that had formerly operated with the Community Fire Safety Division. This unit carried the new boat and a Rigid Inflatable boat.

The brigade's new boat was designed especially for rescue purposes and is pictured in the River Tyne just off Newcastle Quayside in May 2006.

After just over twenty years of service the original West Denton incident command unit was replaced in 2003 by a smart new unit, also based on a Dennis chassis. The appliance responded to all calls that required six or more pumps, as occurred at Cape Insulations, Washington, in June 2003.

Sunderland Central Fire Station was built in 1908, a time when the police were responsible for the fire and ambulance services. The station closed in 1993 upon the opening of a new fire station at Railway Row. The old station was still extant in 2006.

Swalwell Fire Station, built by Durham County Council in 1963, closed in 2006 and was replaced by a new building a few hundred yards further west. The establishment here housed two pumps. (T&WF CDA)

Grindon 1988

Sunderland's Grindon Fire Station closed in 2005, the staff and appliances relocating to North Moor Lane together with the personnel from Tunstall Fire Station. Within weeks of closing the station was demolished and housing built on the site. (T. Welham)

Washington Fire Station was built in 1971 and incorporated housing for the ten firefighters who were to operate on a day-manning system. When this manning arrangement was not pursued, the station was extended. It closed in October 2005 when a new combined fire and ambulance station was opened at Sulgrave.

The central police and fire station at Keppel Street in South Shields, pictured in 1986. This station served the town well for over seventy years until it was replaced by a new community fire station on John Reid Road. Upon its closure the premises were quickly demolished and retail shops built on the site. (T. Welham)

In 2003 the four north-eastern fire and rescue services, Cleveland, Durham, Northumberland and Tyne & Wear, united under the auspices of the North East Strategic Partnership Board for purchasing fire engines. Under this new body they purchased a series of appliances based on Dennis Sabre chassis with bodywork by Excalibur. Washington received this example in 2004.

Almost all of the early fire engines described in this book have been scrapped, but it is gratifying to know that Tyne & Wear Fire & Rescue Service has continued to support the preservation of some old appliances, notably this 1951 Dennis F12 pump escape from Tynemouth Fire Brigade.

Other local titles published by Tempus

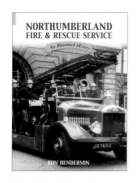

Northumberland Fire & Rescue Service

RON HENDERSON

As with all Britain's counties, the population of Northumberland is greatly dependent on the efficiency and professionalism of its fire brigade.

From its inception in 1948 to the present day, this is a tribute to all the people who have made the Brigade so successful and features over 150 old and recent photographs.

978 0 7524 3540 4

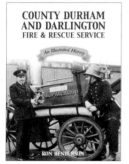

County Durham and Darlington Fire & Rescue Service

RON HENDERSON

The County Durham and Darlington Fire & Rescue Service is responsible for affording fire protection to a population of just over half a million people and remains an invaluable force in the area

This book features over 150 archive and modern photographs of the County Durham Fire & Rescue Service over the years, beginning with its inception in 1948 up to the present day.

978 0 7524 4179 5

Firefighting in Worcestershire

CLIVE SHEARMAN

In 1666 Government decreed that every parish should maintain a fire engine and the first record of one in Worcestershire dates from 1700. By the 1900s, each town had its own brigade or relied on the services of nearby engines. After the Second World War, the Fire Service we know and recognise today was formed.

This book tells the story of firefighting in the county, showing the men, the engines, the fires and the other disasters they encountered.

978 0 7524 3166 6

Firefighting in Kent

JOHN A. MEAKINS & ROGER C. MARDON

Firefighting was initially a community affair driven by survival instincts. It was not until the nineteenth century that fire brigades were formed in Kent.

This book traces the story of this fascinating development, complemented by over 200 photographs of fire engines, brigades, street scenes, and architecture. It will interest local people, historians, and fire service and vehicle enthusiasts.

978 0 7524 3260 1

If you are interested in purchasing other books published by Tempus, or in case you have difficulty finding any Tempus books in your local bookshop, you can also place orders directly through our website

www.tempus-publishing.com